China's Underground Catholic Church "Realities"

Introduction

I once thought of China as a world away. I thought whatever was going on there was none of my affair. I didn't know anything about their government or the struggles of their people. I was totally in touch with my simple little safety zone, the one of only my small world. I have grown up here in midsized city USA, safe from many terrible things that our Christian brothers and sisters in other parts of the world do not take for granted. This is a brief out-line of a two week mission trip to China. Many things are vague for the protection of those walking a very difficult path in a difficult world.

Dedication

Picture a room where there are on any given day 40-50 new born babies. In this particular room there are only two workers to care for the infants. They work a very tough 12 hour shift and then lock the doors and go home, leaving the babies to bare life alone for the next 12 hours. The next morning they move the dead and dying ones to the hospice side of the room where death awaits them. Soon their bodies are taken to the incinerator.

This book is dedicated to all of those children who die in countries such as China where there is no protection for the unborn and limited protection for the newly born. May the Lord bless each one of these children and may the world come to learn their value. At the very moment that you are reading this many are struggling for their last breath. Please add these children to your prayer list and better yet say a prayer for them now. Thank you.

Hearing God's call in China

Chapter 1

A few months back I was leading a small prayer group at St. Mary's which I have attended since childhood. The Thursday night prayer meeting was much like any other. We sang and praised our Lord, we invited the Holy Spirit to rest upon us and open our eyes to each other's needs and there was a short teaching I had prepared on "Expanding the Circumference of Our Lives." It's a teaching that takes many forms and I have heard different versions from many sources, it's really nothing new.

The teaching has to do with the many ways in which we hear God's calling in our lives - through friends, scripture, dreams, visions, prompting of the Spirit, through wonderful things in our lives and even through very unpleasant circumstances. Toward the end of the teaching I challenged the prayer group's 18 or so members to step out in faith in the following days to see what God wanted from them.

I had absolutely no idea what lay in store. The next morning I attended the 7:00am Mass as usual. A close friend of mine, Sister Rita, asked if she could have a private word with me. I assumed it would be over some monetary need that the Sisters of this local community were in need of. Much to my surprise she quietly asked if I would give a friend of hers a call. She explained that her friend was a missionary and that he was going to China soon to visit with the underground Roman Catholic Church. She went on to tell me that he had called her asking for help on locating someone to accompany him on his upcoming trip. Sister Rita said, "This morning I was in prayer and when I asked for the Lord's guidance on a name for him, yours kept coming up."

I was more than a little surprised. I have no experience in missionary work. I had absolutely no desire to visit China and really believed that she was probably just misled. That morning during Mass I prayed and asked God what He wanted from me. Immediately the teaching from the night before came into focus. It was then that I remembered my own words of "Hear the other side of the conversation; let God speak to you this week." Chills went through me. I dismissed the thought and as I stuck my hand inside of my pocket I felt the small piece of paper on which Sister Rita had written the man's name and phone number.

Later at work I sat at my desk and I looked at the number and thought to myself, "what harm could it be, I will just call and visit with him." I did, and he seemed like a very caring man, a man of God. I asked him several questions and we exchanged email addresses. He gave me several requirements such as the trip would last several weeks, it would start in just six weeks, I would need a passport, Visa, and such. The cost would be approximately $2,700.00 and I should bring a digital camera if possible.

As I hung up I asked the Lord very quietly, "Is this something you want of me? If so, make it known without a doubt." Afterwards I contacted my wife and told her of the events. She knows that I am very uncomfortable in traveling to new destinations, that I have my comfort zone. She is also aware of my procrastination and stubbornness.

I felt an urgency to check my passport to see if it was valid, it wasn't. I breathed a sigh of relief and went online to see how long it would take to get it renewed. Two to three weeks, great, this was probably my way out. I did send it in anyway and received a tracking number of sorts. Good, that was out of the way.

Meanwhile my wife had been visiting with Sister Rita about this situation, asking her all sorts of questions about her reasons for having asked me to consider this trip. That night she smiled at me and said, "I believe you should look seriously at this, if God says no, don't force it, if he says yes, ask him again. Keep checking to see if this really is HIS will." We knew very little about the "Underground" Roman Catholic Church in China. It sounded a bit alarming.

It was two weeks later that I received my passport back, so the next step was the Visa. I sent it off - maybe this would be the stumbling block. Meanwhile I looked over our finances. I knew that $2,700.00 was a lot to use for my personal journey. I also quickly realized that I had been looking at building a shed in the back of our property that would cost right at $2,700.00. I knew the answer to this. God really didn't care if I had a place to store my excess junk. The guilt trip quickly formed in my head. Would I put a chance to help my brothers and sisters in Christ second to my wanting an extra place to store material goods that should have already been dispersed to others? A phrase my mother taught me went through my head: "Often times a mortal sin may be the extra jacket we keep in our closet, while somewhere someone is freezing." Okay the money was solved.

Soon I received notice that my Visa was approved and had been sent by overnight means and would be here the next day. Everything was falling in place.

The missionary and I chatted again. This time he informed me of our itinerary. It began to take shape in my head just what was being asked of me. We only had a few details on our travel. What we were doing was completely illegal. China does not permit foreign missionaries, especially from the Roman Catholic Church. They also see Charismatic Catholics as a religious cult and do not want any outsiders spreading any such messages of Charisms and such. While surfing the web I read one article about a house Mass where local officials of the Chinese Government had raided the apartment during the Mass and had thrown 4-5 individuals off of the 6th floor balcony. This had been done to discourage others from any form of worship outside of a government approved building. There were also many articles on the sufferings of Catholics in China, many of the imprisonment of clergy and of labor camps. It seemed strange that this was not something that was ever concentrated on by the free press. But there were too many facts to ignore. This could obviously be a dangerous situation.

I was notified that our contact in Beijing, Sister X, would not be able to provide us with much information on what our agenda would consist of. Since she runs a home for pregnant mothers that are in hiding from the Population Police, she is under constant scrutiny. Her emails and phone calls are watched very carefully by the government, so she would not and could not convey much information.

I was contacted again by the missionary, almost everything was in place. Then a friend of mine asked me if there was anything I need for my trip. I explained that almost everything was taken care of with the exception of a digital camera and my boss's permission. This wonderful gentleman gave me a check for a very nice digital movie camera.

The next day I visited with my boss. He is not always open to religious excursions. His wife has done many hours of community service and he has witnessed the effects of people getting so involved in church activities that their family life and careers suffer. I could hardly have blamed him if he had a bad reaction to my going. At the time I was well into my 2nd year in the deaconate training to become a permanent deacon in the Catholic Church. He knew I was spending some weekends and lots of weekdays on studying and preparing for this thing he saw as a major change in my life.

So on a Monday morning I entered his office and closed the door. I explained that I felt very called to follow through on this mission trip. I went over all of the obstacles that had been removed. I assured him that I would cover my work to the best of my ability before and after this 20 day trip. He didn't hesitate at all. He said if you feel that strongly that you need to go, go. I'll do what it takes to cover you while you are gone.

Everything was in place. I received an email from the missionary outlining what little he knew of the scheduling. We would arrive in Beijing and from there someone would meet with us and transport us by car to an undisclosed location. We would spend several days getting acclimated to the time change while we prepared for a week long seminar to be given to a large number of underground Prayer Groups. I was asked how comfortable I was in giving teachings and in praying hands-on with individuals in need. Since I have led a prayer group for several years and had some training on teachings through the National Service Committee and the deaconate, I agreed to do whatever was asked of me. He then went on to explain that we would be meeting with at least two Bishops and maybe others. Things were a little sketchy. We planned on leaving our separate home states and meeting in New York and then flying off to Beijing.

In the days to come I asked the Lord to prepare me, to help me understand His will in my life. I contemplated what it must have been like for the apostles to have left home going to foreign places, places where they would be in jeopardy of physical harm and imprisonment. I wondered what reasons He could have for wanting me to visit such a distant country. I decided to go to confession the day before I was scheduled to leave, and then to go knowing that HE was in charge. My biggest fear was disappointing HIM.

I visited with a friend's friend, who explained to me his past experiences in China. He made the statement that often he had been driven around in the back seat of a car, hiding from cameras which seemed to be everywhere in

China. He warned that many people who are caught must sign a paper apologizing to the Chinese Government and declare their disbelief in God. He stated that this is done to keep people in line. He added if a person was going to be doing a mission they must decide their own beliefs on signing such a paper. He said many have signed to get permission to leave the country and that many have been tortured into signing such a document. Some have just been expelled from the country while still others have been beaten and dropped off in the Philippians.

I would later find out that a phrase I was to hear could not have been more true, "Much of what you will hear about China will be contradictory, and seem impossible, but will be true somewhere in China."

I decided that increasing my adoration time in front of the Eucharist along with an increase in my prayer time was definitely in order.

Chapter 2

I stepped off of the plane in New York and found my new friend, the missionary, waiting on me with a warm smile on his face. We introduced ourselves over lunch and spent a few moments getting to know each other. It would be a 14+ hour trip and we would have more time in Beijing for small talk.

It was on the plane just moments before landing when the missionary gave me the following instructions. "I am sort of well known since I have been a missionary for 28 years. I have only made one other trip to China, so keep the $2,000.00 in cash that I asked you to bring, in a safe place. When we go through customs keep your distance from me. If they should stop me, or look on my laptop, there are 1,500 hours of teachings that will give me away. Or, they may just know who I am and that I am coming. If they stop me, proceed on like you don't know me. Sister X will be looking for you in the airport and will take you with her. Don't look back, don't worry about me. Just go do the mission work she has outlined for us."

This was a bit of a twist. Of course it is not like there is a travel guide you can read on things to prepare for when doing missionary work in China. I will admit to having been a bit surprised, but figured HE brought me this far, so let us walk the walk.

Once again, in the pages that follow I will be very vague on places and names and often on things that might give away who I am relating the story about. The people we met who helped us and setup the mission would be in grave danger should the Chinese Government identify them.

We passed by a line in customs where travelers were busy running their baggage through an X-ray machine. The missionary said follow me quickly and we walked past everyone in line and just pretended to know where we were going and what we were doing. Through a corridor and up some stairs and we were in Beijing, no questions asked. We had just walked completely through the customs area. And there we met Sister X. She is a small woman, although of obvious later years, is full of energy and has as much or more faith than anyone I have ever known.

We were escorted to a "black taxi". I was informed that a "black taxi" is an individual who is not a legal taxi according to the government. These are men and women who use their cars to transport people for pay, but at a lower rate than the legal taxis which are often bugged and have drivers that will turn foreigners into the government for discussing forbidden, or suspicious topics. It was a very smoggy day, so much pollution that the mountains and the Great Wall could not be seen. We were taken to what appeared to be an apartment complex. Much like one would expect to see in a large city, only there were guards at the gate, and the driver had to stop and check in with them upon entering.

We lugged our luggage up the cold flights of stairs to an apartment Sister X uses for an office and for guests. She was so warm, so nice, you could feel the love and devotion of God even in her glance. The room was filled with information on ProLife issues. Some of the information was in Chinese and some was in English. There were bookshelves filled with Catholic and religious titles, a small out of date computer and some comforts of home. There were two bedrooms and a room setup as a chapel. We would spend our first few days here teaching several mothers some Catholic teachings, but mostly just admiring their babies. We would later find out that most men in China have a great dislike for these very women because of their children. Since many people are taught at an early age abortion is nothing more than a quick necessary procedure and it is a normal fact of life for the Chinese people, to have children (plural) or to have a child out of wedlock is a disgraceful terrible thing, and the mothers are then often abandoned by their families and even by their husbands.

Chapter 3

The following story was related to us of one of the mothers (we will call her Kay):

Kay was born in a poor village. Her father died when she was 15 and in her 2nd year of middle school. After her father died Kay had to quit school and work in the fields. Shortly before her father died, Kay's mother, Brea (alias), had finished her abortion training in the hospital and began this work for the government. Her clientele gradually increased over the years. Kay used to help her though all the blood frightened her.

When she was 21, Kay married. Their village was extremely poor. They had one son. Kay became pregnant again the next year. Due to the very stringent one child per family policy and the ruthless methods used to enforce it in their area, this pregnancy was terminated by Kay's mother. A subsequent 3rd pregnancy two years later was also aborted by the grandmother.

Now in those days the government family planning policy was implemented very stringently in their village. The officials in their area were responsible to the higher officials in the other areas. The officials in those areas were responsible to those higher officials in the **XXXX**. The officials used to come around regularly and collect fines from those who were pregnant without permission and escort them to the abortion facilities. They would also conduct mandatory sonograms every three months for all married women under the age of 40. If a woman failed to show up, she would be fined. If they didn't pay the fine either the woman herself or, if she was absent, then her parents, her husband or the husband's parents (whatever relative was available) would be tied with their hands behind their back and taken to the village center where many people congregated selling things. They would be tied to a light pole or a tree and have to stand for many hours. If, during that time, they had to use the bathroom, they were escorted by two people. Most people paid the fine to be released. At other times, they are taken to the local police station and kept there but not given any food. Some pay the fine. Others have stayed as much as two weeks. When higher officials such as those in the **XXXX** came around, the officials in the area used to warn the people who were not cooperating with them and tell them to hide. This is because if the **XXXX** officials found someone pregnant without permission, the area officials would lose their jobs. The policies were enforced so stringently because this was an extremely poor village and the family planning officials used to pocket some of the fine money. The same thing happened at the level of the **XXXX** when they would be inspected by the higher governmental officials.

When Kay became pregnant for the fourth time, she did not tell her mother right away. Nevertheless, she was subjected to the compulsory sonogram when she was one month along. The pregnancy was not discovered. Again when she was between four and five months, she was again subjected to the compulsory sonogram. Two health workers looked at the sonogram and they miraculously reported there was no pregnancy; however, they did report that there was something unusual—maybe a tumor. When Kay returned home from this finding, her mother massaged her abdomen thoroughly. Kay reports that her mother was so very skilled in this technique which she mastered to detect pregnancies, that she could, in this manner, detect pregnancies at only 45 days gestation. Well, this time her mother also did not discover this pregnancy but did detect something unusual and took Kay to another clinic where a sonogram confirmed the pregnancy. At this point, the mother discovered that her daughter had been dishonest with her and was very angry (and extremely frightened of the family planning officials---so much so that she developed heart trouble from that time.) She took her home and began to perform the abortion by administering 20 bottles of suogongsu to induce delivery but all was without success. Nothing happened. Then the mother performed acupuncture on those body parts which would induce contractions. Again, this also was unsuccessful. Then, in desperation and fright, she took Kay to a big hospital. Pregnancy was again confirmed and the abortion was in process of being scheduled when blood tests revealed that Kay had hepatitis and was anemic. Hospitals fear hepatitis and will not perform abortions on women with hepatitis for fear of contracting it themselves. So they sent her home. Kay and her mother knew that, if she returned home, she would be fined by the family planning officials and so they went to a nearby village. When Kay was 8 months, her mother, being petrified of the officials, administered medicine to her daughter which brought on early contractions and she thus delivered the baby prematurely. This baby turned out to be a healthy son.

When this child was born, Kay immediately returned to her village leaving the son in the care of friends who bottle fed him. Now at that time, the younger brother of Kay's husband who is the principal of a school and considered quite intelligent recommended that they go to a clinic where he had some connections, and ask for the body of a large aborted fetus. This done, they returned home and when the officials came they showed them the dead baby girl fetus saying that it was their daughter who had died. The officials then departed satisfied.

In the meantime, in the other village where the baby was, word was going around that a baby boy was born. Someone offered to pay 10,000 RMB (about US$1479) for the child. The maternal grandmother was hoping they would sell but the parents refused. (Now, baby boys are bought for 100,000 RMB.)

At that time, a friend went to the family planning officials in XXXX and asked if a woman whose baby had died could nurse a baby from their village. They said that would be acceptable. So the baby was brought to Kay's house, her own baby, and she nursed him for about a year. During this time, neighbors used to come around and say: "My, this baby does resemble your husband." It would always be denied that it was their baby. After about a year, the officials found out and severely fined them.

The family planning officials used to come frequently to their village and announce over the loudspeakers the names of those they were looking for. Kay's sons used to hear these announcements and panic. They used to go and hide in the fields if it was summer or, in winter, they would not open their gate and pretend they were not home. Sometimes, Kay would hide her second son in a vegetable basket attached to her bike. Although the officials from the areas knew Kay well and she could not fool them, when the officials from the XXXX would come, Kay would pretend that she was not who they thought she was. She was her husband's younger sister or cousin etc.

In 2004, Kay, her husband, mother and all the children were baptized into the Catholic Church. After that, in 2005, after nine years of no live births, Kay became pregnant. Since she was a Catholic, she refused to have an abortion. Her mother was disgusted and asked her why she didn't have an abortion like all the other Catholic women who were her clients. When Kay persisted in her refusal to undergo an abortion, her mother, in disgust, ripped off the medal from her neck and threw it on the floor and said if this is what it meant to be a Catholic then she didn't want to be one. Kay's husband, busy tending the fields, seldom went to church.

Although Kay refused the abortion, she was extremely frightened by the family planning officials and hid in the house saying 4-5 rosaries a day. Another woman, a devout Catholic, had told her not to be frightened that Blessed Mother would protect her. She told her the story about how the family planning officials were in the process of taking one woman away for a forced abortion. This woman was very devoted to Our Lady. As she was being taken away, the officials suddenly couldn't find her. She had, rather miraculously disappeared out of their midst. Much like Jesus did when people were attempting to throw Him over the cliff in Nazareth.

At four months into this pregnancy, a friend of Kay's went to the hospital and offered the doctor 100 RMB. In return, he issued numerous false health reports stating that Kay had hepatitis, kidney disease, heart problems etc. and so the clinic did not want to do the abortion.

Kay continued to keep their gate closed and pretend that no one was home. However, when she was six months along, one day her husband was moving a pile of fertilizer from their compound to the field and forgot to close the gate. Within 15 minutes, it had been reported to the family planning officials that the gate was open and they appeared and arrested Kay stating that the previous health reports were false. They took her to the office where they kept her-- demanding that they pay a fine of 2000 RMB. They said that Kay could get the money back after she had her abortion. Finally, at around 11:00pm they gave the 2,000 RMB, but again, she chose not to abort.

The officials continued to knock on their gate during the following months. Kay would stay inside and pretend no one was home and would pray rosary after rosary. She was very frightened and could not go out except after dark.

As the day of the birth drew near, Kay's husband and mother were angry and refused to stay home to help with the birth stating that they must go out to the fields to work. They left but later a mighty wind came forcing them to return home. Kay had really no labor time. She was busy preparing mantou (steamed bread) and doing laundry when it was time for the baby to be born. The mother came in time to assist with the birth. The father came just as she was giving birth. They were all relieved that it was a girl. This was because boys cost money when they grow up. When they marry, they have to provide a place to live and many other things which are a very great burden on a poor family. Soon after this birth, the family planning officials heard about it and came around to the house.

Thank heavens this little baby girl did not cry. Now they had to hide the newly washed diapers and could not hang them out to dry in full view of the neighbors or family planning officials who might be passing by. They had to hang them in hidden places.

During this pregnancy, Kay's stomach was very big. The neighbors all said it would be a boy. When she had a girl, they accused her of exchanging her boy with someone else who had a girl. They refused to believe that it was her baby.

One year recently, Kay became pregnant for the 6th time. Once again, because she was Catholic, she did not want an abortion. She was very frightened but trusted in Our Lady.

Some Sisters introduced her to a safe home away from her village. No one in the family wanted this baby. Everyone was disgusted with Kay.

On Holy Thursday night very late, Kay's labor began and she went to the hospital. She was very honest and told them this was her 4th child. The staff all treated her with a very bad attitude. No one could be with her that night. Finally, on Good Friday in the early morning about 6:30 she delivered a beautiful baby boy so effortlessly and so quickly that the doctor was not present at the moment and scolded her, even slapped her!

Now if she was insisting on giving birth to the baby, the husband and mother wanted a girl because they are less expensive than a boy especially when they marry—boys have to provide a lot which is a burden for a poor family. When Kay's husband came to the hospital to sign for the birth certificate, he gave a look of disgust at Kay because she had given birth to a boy and walked out. Kay's mother helped around the safe house for a week or two but paid more attention to another little baby girl that was there than to her own grandson. Before she left to return to the countryside, she told her daughter just to put the baby out on the street.

It is especially appropriate that Providence chose Good Friday as the day on which this little boy should be born. Jesus was crucified on Good Friday. No one except His Mother stood by him. What will become of this little boy called *****? It reminds one of the scripture verse: "The stone that was rejected has become the cornerstone." Will this little boy one day become a priest? Or a great father of a family? God only knows. But it is a miracle that he was born at all!

An American friend of the safe house was visiting recently and left a donation of U.S. dollars to Kay for her baby.

Kay did not want to take it. However, it was explained to her that this was not her money but rather *****'s. She accepted it.

In the meantime, word had gone around that Kay had given birth to a baby boy. There were many offers to buy the child for 10,000 RMB. Family members, including Kay's mother, sister and others (husband wavering) were putting a lot of pressure on Kay to sell and get rid of this baby. Because an American friend had given her a donation, Kay was able to reply saying that God had already shown His Providential care for this baby and that He wants us to trust Him to provide for the future as well.

It is Kay's greatest desire to go home and be with her family. However, this cannot be for the present. So she is seeking a safe place to go with her daughter and baby boy. In the meantime, they are in hiding. Please pray for them.

This is only one of many stories. One young lady told us that her husband was so ashamed that she was pregnant for the second time that he had disowned her. Her baby girl was just several weeks old, but she had already decided that it was best if the baby girl was raised as a boy. She said she was going to keep her hair cut short and call her by a boy's name. And that she would even dress her as a boy as she grew so that she would be thought of as having some worth in Chinese Society. She also told us of how her husband had offered for her to rejoin him and his new wife as their maid/servant. She said that it was her only choice and that she was going to comply.

Chapter 4

We enjoyed our stay and even attended communion services every day, or went to a local friend's house where House Masses were said four times a week. The time came four days into our journey to travel to a destination well within the poorer areas of China, miles from the hustle of Beijing. We border a fast train and headed hours from the city. We arrived in a small town where we were met by an underground Priest, Father A, and an underground Sister, Sister C. These two who posed as a couple did not speak any English. We were taken to their car and headed off, knowing that we had to trust them, even though we had never met them.

We arrived at an apartment much like the one we had left, only this one was in a smaller town and somewhat newer. A Sister awaited us that is to be our translator. Her name was Sister B. Sister B is a lovely young lady by anyone's standard. She has a very charming smile and laughs often. We quickly fell in love with her and all of the Sisters of this underground group. We were informed that a five day conference would be held in a few days. They asked that in the meantime we give them two days of teachings. The missionary took the first day and did some biblical teachings, comparing different parts of the Bible with our current time in history. I took the second day, telling them first my testimony then relating some true stories of modern day Christians who I have been fortunate enough to meet. I was unaware of why these sisters and two priests (we had been joined by another) seemed to hang on my words. They seemed so fully engulfed in my stories.

In the mornings I would look out through the large patio windows on the 6th floor of the complex and see the workers next door. They were construction workers going about their busy day constructing yet another apartment complex. These complexes are numerous, and many of them are sectioned off with an 8' tall fence that has razor wire on the top. There are numerous cameras and only a few entrances and exits. When entering or leaving the driver must always stop and address the guard, who seemed to be a government employee dressed in military attire.

On our third morning, I looked out on the construction sight to see military personnel questioning the workers. Within a few moments they were pointing up towards our apartment. I will admit that it was at this very moment that I started to pray for protection. Not just for us, but for the Sisters and two Priests. I shared this with Sister B, our interpreter; she smiled and shrugged her shoulders. We all ate in a hurry, and then proceeded outside to several waiting cars. We drove for several miles and then down several small alley ways. We pulled up to a gate and the priest driving honked the horn. A small man appeared and opened the large gate. As we pulled inside we could see a small class room type building, much like a one room school house with a loading dock outside. We could hear singing and Chinese worship songs being sung inside.

We exited the cars and were quickly ushered into the back of the building. There seemed to be quite a buzz of excitement about our arrival. Then we were ushered onto a stage area at one end of the classroom. Everyone started applauding. This was quite new to me. I haven't spoken in many public forums, and this was a definitely a new experience. Sister B introduced the missionary and me. The room erupted in applause again. The Sisters started to sing praise and worship songs, then another, then the entire room broke out in a beautiful singing in the Spirit. Approximately 60-70 Chinese people praying and singing in tongues. What a moment.

Afterwards, the Missionary opened us up with a prayer. He taught for two hours on the Holy Scripture. I was not entirely impressed with his mannerism or teaching abilities, but was with his knowledge of Scripture. After two hours, he and the interpreter took a well deserved break and they asked if I would give the next two hours of teaching. I was a little nervous and asked the Holy Spirit to lead the session. I prayed that no matter what I said, HE would let them hear what they needed to hear. He answered my prayer.

These beautiful Chinese people, many with hard looks and aged beyond their years, listened intently to me tell stories of Catholic faith. One teaching was on how I came to be in China, increasing your circumference. That afternoon's teaching was on "Sandy- Salvation in Motion" about a courageous woman dying of cancer who received the miracle of her family growing closer to God through her losing fight with this horrible disease.

After my second teaching one of the Sisters who spoke very little English enlisted the interpreter to speak with me. She asked how I knew what the people so desperately needed to hear. I asked her what she meant. I was confused by her question. She told me they liked hearing the missionary speak of biblical stories, but the Chinese people are a people of traditional story telling. Many had traveled for 1,000 miles or more, and they could be imprisoned or physically harmed for even attending this seminar. She then asked how soon I would be speaking again. I was so shocked. I had really believed up to this moment that I was just more or less filler. The Lord made it very apparent that these people were starved to hear of people in other countries who shared the same struggles in life. So I shared on life struggles, hearing God's word in our daily lives, a story of three men from different backgrounds who find God in their lives and of my own personal walk with Christ. After the five days were completed we had grown as a group to around 200 people. Some stood outside of the doors and windows and took notes.

During the seminar, once we were asked to all turn off our cell phones. The priest explained that the local Bishop had been arrested again. He asked that all the participants leave in different directions at the end of the day. We also notice that the guards to the complex we were staying in had been changed from government employees, to armed military police.

Several things happened during this seminar/conference that has increased my faith a 100 fold and I would like to share them.

1. While praying for the group, the missionary asked me to walk among the crowded room and pray for whoever seemed in need of healing prayer. I followed his instruction and walked along the center aisle. There were several I prayed with, but one lady toward the back caught my eye. She seemed somehow different than the rest. She was very short and had eyes that were so covered with cataracts that she couldn't have seen very well, if any at all. Her hands were in a cupped position and the skin was so dried and

hard that they wouldn't even bend. I took these precious hands in mine and began to pray. I felt an extreme amount of heat coming from them and ended by leaning forward and kissing each hand. Then I lightly ran my hand along her cheek and said thank you for your years of work. As I released her hands the man next to her grabbed my hands and pulled them to his chest. He leaned into them and started to stare at me with total hate in his eyes. I smiled gently at him and prayed in the Spirit. His eyes started to roll back into his head and he started to belch loudly. I stared intently at him wondering what it was that he was being released from. The belching got louder then started to subside. The people around him had all backed away. I nodded for them to come closer and pray with him, but they shook their heads "no." I finally grabbed a man close to me and pulled him forward as I prayed louder. He put his hands on the man and started to pray also, we were quickly joined by many others. This man we prayed for fell back into the chair behind him and seemed to fall asleep. The next day I was informed that it scared those present because he was their local priest.

2. On the third day of this seminar, I was praying for several people. One, a tall slender older woman reached out to me. I took her hands and began to pray in the Spirit. I had closed my eyes and felt a need to open them. When I did and looked at her, her eyes were closed and she seemed so very

relaxed. She was also praying in the Spirit. I felt prompted so I asked in my mind only, as I continued praying in the Spirit, and in my mind I said, "Open your eyes." She did. Now I do not speak Chinese nor does she speak English, and I only said it in my mind. But she had heard me, or had she. My doubt was present. I continued on and once again in my mind only I asked, "Do you know that Christ is your Savior, that He walks the earth today looking for souls to claim, just as He did when he was a man?" She looked puzzled, but shook her head "yes." Then as I felt prompted to do so I asked, "Do you believe in God with all your heart and mind?" Again she shook her head "yes." I stared at her hardly able to believe what the Holy Spirit was doing. I asked one final question (remember these were only asked in my mind), "Do you do now and have you always done what the Lord asks of you?" She began to shake and tears began to pour down from her eyes. Her lips quivered as she leaned forward and collapsed into my arms. I sat her gently into her chair.

3. Several of us gathered around a young woman who said that she had some sort of infection in her throat. It had bothered her for several years. We prayed for her and as we did my mouth began to fill with a horrible tasting liquid. It was hard to pray, then it seemed to evaporate and she started to vomit up a horrible smelling liquid. Afterwards she said that the pain in her throat had gone.

I do not claim to understand all that happened. I just know that it did happen and there were witnesses.

The woman described in #3 above told us the following story: She said when she was younger (now 40+) she did not like her husband very much. He used a typical method of training on her. He would lay her down on the floor, kneel beside her and break several of her ribs by kicking her with his knee. He would then apply slight pressure to her broken rib/ribs whenever she disobeyed; also admitting he had broken her nose, split her lips and caused many other injuries to her. This was done along with other humiliations to make her a good wife. She said now he has been converted and no long breaks her ribs, but he still beats her if she does not satisfy him. I asked why she did not divorce him and she looked puzzled. She answered, "Where would I go, what would I do. I could leave him, but here the man gets everything. I have no legal right to leave him. All of my relatives and his would then hate me for bringing disgrace on our families."

The seminar/conference ended. I have never spent so much time in prayer with a group, or with so many one on one. It was a very blessed event and the memories of the faces, the gentleness and prayerfulness of these people I will never forget.

Chapter 5

We headed off from the Sisters apartment the next morning. I was a bit sad to leave my new friends. These Sisters will forever be in my heart and in my prayers. We were driven by one of the priest several hours to meet alongside the road with a man I will call Mr. G. This Mr. G. has several priests in his family. He has even been through the seminary himself, but knows should he be ordained, he will no longer be allowed to travel in and out of China. He visited with us briefly and then we were off to meet with one of the Bishops that had requested our visitation. We arrived at a location I will not describe here because it may bring hardships upon this blessed Bishop.

When we arrived at his residence we were escorted to his main sitting room. He stood politely and through the interpreter introduced himself. He then abruptly ended our meeting and the interpreter explained he had other more pressing business and we were to go to freshen up and take a nap. So we were ushered down the hall to a bathroom area. We washed our hands and then were escorted through a back hallway to a large bedroom where the Bishop was sitting on the bed. He explained his office had government cameras and microphones in it and here we could visit in seclusion. He told us a story of his captivity, of his escape and of having received many punishments in the past years. He implored us to tell others to come and evangelize in China, to as our Pope has proclaimed "Do not be afraid." This blessed man visited for several hours with us. He told of the government policies against the teaching of religious classes to children of school age. He said this is to help ignorance flourish, to eventually eliminate religious thoughts in the people's minds. He stated the government wants people to be more secularized, to depend upon their monies and the government, not on God. He looked very distant and sad as he explained that it's working on our young people.

I cannot go into much of the interview for fear it would make him recognizable should a government official read this text. I will say he has suffered greatly and so have his Sisters and Priests under his care.

We were then led to an ambulance so we could travel unnoticed and in comfort to another Diocese several hours away. Soon we arrived at a very underdeveloped set of ancient buildings in need of much repair. This Bishop, who lives in an extremely very modest surrounding, showed us a picture of a lavish beautiful Cathedral. He explained while his church building is now very bare and small, he once had a very fine Cathedral, but the local government officials had removed him and his parish from it in order to make it a government building. He says with pain in his voice. "They gave me this small piece of land and said now start again." So he has. We spent the evening with about 18 priests of all ages. They were a very inquisitive group. Many asked why we had come, what our mission was and the like. They were obviously men of God.

One of the Priest that we met, Father Q, told us his story: He was born in the 60's and his mother and father both taught RCIA classes in their home. They had been warned repeatedly by the local officials to stop. First his father was arrested then let out of prison, later he was arrested again on the same charge. Within several months he died in prison. His mother had now taken over giving the RCIA classes. Soon she was arrested and soon released. During this time period, the church they attended had been attacked by the local government. One Sunday while they were away visiting relatives, the military police had come and boarded up the church doors and windows during the Sunday service and set the church on fire, many of his family and friends had been in that church.

Yet his mother persisted in teaching the RCIA classes at their home. Soon she was arrested again and this time died in prison. Father Q was placed with his aunt and uncle, who were also devout Catholics. Soon his uncle, who he described as a large man, was arrested on the same charges. He would only spend a few days in prison and then was released after he signed a paper stating that he no longer believed in God and he would no longer give classes or pray. He came back home, but could not eat, drink or sleep. After several days at home, he said his goodbyes to his family and returned to prison. He demanded that his papers be torn up and he be allowed to enter the prison, they obliged and he was dead within six months. When Father Q went with his aunt to claim the body, they were shown a plywood box that was screwed shut. His aunt persisted that she could not claim a box without seeing what was inside of it. So they opened the box. Inside they saw his uncle, now a very thin man. His arms and thighs had been bound with something that had cut off the circulation and his arms and legs had rotted off of him while he was still alive. They had used an axe to chop open his chest and remove his heart in hopes it would stop any afterlife. It was then Father Q says he vowed to become a priest.

He attended a Political Church Seminary and hoped since it was in legal standing he could at least help people to understand God. Upon his ordination he was told since his family had been such a bother to the government, he would not be allowed to act as a priest. So he was now let go into the streets - not allowed to function as a priest nor allowed to seek employment either. He said this is why he disappeared into the underground network of priests. He sheds many tears while telling his story and I shall never forget his face, or his courage.

Before we left, the Bishop asked if we could return and give seminars to his clergy and religious sisters. He said he would be in touch, and for us to keep him in our prayers. He has been arrested on many occasions. We headed off from there late at night for a train station that would take us back toward Beijing.

Chapter 6

Back in Beijing, the hustle and bustle of the touristy city. One would never understand or know what lies just outside of this city, the fear of its people, or the dictatorship of its government. From the view here there is not much of a thought of the communist mindset. Not much is known by tourists of the population police, of forced abortions. There is not much mention of dying rooms where babies that are not perfect because of a clubbed foot, or even a minor deformity are signed away by their blood parents and sent off to a room to be denied medical treatment, food and water until they cease to be alive. No this is a beautiful city, one that does not show its real self for fear of being denied some privilege supported by the economics of a world that would rather look the other way then have to face this nation of three billion people.

Some things we should know about China:

1. Like any country it has many wonderful people.
2. It has more people now than any other nation has ever had in the history of the world (over three billion).
3. China's government has less respect for life then any country in existence today.
4. China's roads even in smaller cities are 6-8 lanes wide and have lights off to the sides so that they can be easily converted to landing strips for when the next world war starts. They ARE planning on one.

5. China has less freedom of religion then most nations. People are still beat, tortured and imprisoned for their religious beliefs.

6. Abortion is mandated by the government for many of the women in China. Population Police patrol villages and forcibly inject women with abortion chemicals.

7. Many families who avoid abortion, are punished by having their possessions seized, their work permits revoked and are thrown out homeless into the streets as a warning to others.

8. Children are left to die in "hospice" rooms. Not because of terminal illness, but out of convenience.

9. The government has eyes/cameras everywhere, even in churches. One church we visited had cameras

above all the entrances and smaller cameras with microphones over the confessionals.

Chapter 7

Our next stop was a safe haven for mothers. These beautiful ladies do not even see their own worth. They have been so beat down by the government, the secular society and even their own families. Families and relatives are often punished by the government for the disobedience of any of the women who defy the government's abortion attempts. Even extended family can be attacked by the government, so aunts, uncles and grandparents apply an extreme amount of pressure to the young mothers to abort their children.

The missionary and I were privileged to attend a number of House Masses. These were always in homes of trusted individuals. On several occasions the celebrant was one from my home state which helped me feel quite at ease.

We were asked at one point if we could pray for a Mother Superior, a Sister who leads a group of 60-70 religious sisters. We were honored. The next morning our door bell rang and a woman around middle age entered. She wore a scarf over her head, large sunglasses, a very flashy sports jacket, tight jeans, and tennis shoes. As she entered she quickly zippered up her jacket, removed the sunglasses and introduced herself as Mother M. She quietly explained her dilemma. She said she had traveled for four hours to meet with us for prayer. Since she does not speak English, the Sister that runs the Mothers haven interpreted. She explained she lived with her sisters at the residence of a Bishop of the Underground Catholic Church. Several days earlier the government had come in force and taken control of their facility. They were all (Bishop, Sisters and Priests) under house arrest. She explained that she was so scared for her community's safety. She continued saying that the military men are allowed to watch the Sisters shower, bath, dress and that they have no privacy at all. She explained she had changed clothes with a young cleaning woman in order to escape and come to see us. She said if men look at a women's figure, they do not pay such close attention to her face. We asked her what her biggest need was and she answered prayer for being a good leader. She was afraid she was unable and under qualified to lead her community during such trying times. She conveyed her feelings of depression and of despair. Her eyes were filled with such sadness and she looked like a lost child.

As the missionary began praying for her, he glanced at me and asked if the Spirit was prompting me in any way. I smiled and excused myself. I knew what the Spirit was leading me to do, but did not understand why. I returned with a towel, a pitcher of warm water and a large bowl. I knelt before her and removed her shoes. As I began to wash her feet, I explained as Christ had his feet washed by a lowly woman who was unworthy of his touch, I was unworthy to even wash her feet; she is a wonderful spirit filled woman of God and He cherishes her. I then explained of how Christ washed the disciple's feet. He accepted every mile they had walked, and all that they were, and I thanked her for letting me be Jesus to her. I looked up into her eyes and saw the tears flowing from them. I knew that God had once again touched this wonderful woman's heart.

We prayed with her for several minutes and she asked if we had any advice for her. I closed my eyes and had a vision. I then relayed what I saw - *a beautiful box, inlaid with many gem stones, rubies, mother of pearl, garnets and diamonds. The box was opened and many beautiful white doves were flying from it, glitter falling from their wings.* I explained that I thought God was telling her she is a beautiful vessel of HIS, and from her flows the Holy Spirits graces, blessing all of those around her. She put her arms around me and held me close for a very long moment.

As she left the apartment, I wondered what her journey with Christ held in store for her, and wondered if we would ever meet again. We did meet again on another mission, but that story is for another time. She is quite well and a very strong and confident leader of religious women.

Chapter 8

To understand the truth of just how hard life can be for a religious Sister, I will relate here the story from a more recent mission that was told to my wife and I by a wonderful woman I shall refer to as Sister L. She had asked if we had time to pray with her about her religious call. Of course we agreed. An interpreter was used to relate the following story.

When L was young, one of her uncles became a Priest. He came to her mother and requested since her mother had several children, she should give one to become either a Priest or a religious Sister. Her mother volunteered that between all of her children L was the most obedient and best behaved. So it was agreed that L would be given to the church to become a religious Sister.

L was raised by her family until she was in her mid-late teens. She was taught as a small child that she would become a Sister in the Catholic Church. The decision had been made and she would just accept her fate in life. So when it was time she entered a convent and was trained by the Sisters. Her uncle later became a Bishop. He requested she start her own order. The order dedicated themselves to serving the poor, sick and dying, and orphan children.

The order she had helped start grew to 72 Sisters of Mercy; working hard to improve life in very desolate poor parts of China. She explained many times there was little to eat, but the people often shared with her group enough to sustain them. There was also some help from their dioceses.

One day her uncle the Bishop, who was often arrested, was sentenced to prison where he would later die. She felt very lost and alone. A new Bishop took his place.

This new Bishop (above ground church) had not liked her uncle, so he did not like or want her Order to continue. He ordered them to disband and find husbands, to discontinue living out their vows. The Sisters were very confused and decided to disobey this new Bishop and carry on their vows and their work. The Bishop was very angry and stopped all contributions from reaching them. Many of the Sisters felt betrayed by the Church and left. As their numbers fell, only the ones stronger in their faith remained. Soon they started to be arrested for carrying on their acts of charity.

Sister L described to us that she had been imprisoned many times, sometimes for six months to a year. She said the guards would often beat her and the others. She always prayed that through these beatings she would not become pregnant.

Looking at Sister L, you can see the hurt in her eyes as she tells her life story. Her face is scarred and she seems to be very beat down mentally.

She continued telling us even her Bishop had been in part responsible for her imprisonment. At one point someone had notified the acting Papal Nuncio of China, and he had demanded that her and the few Sisters remaining of her Order be treated with respect and be given funds supplied by the Vatican. But the Bishop ignored him. Now, there are only six Sisters remaining of the 72 Sisters.

Sister L asked us, "Why would God allow this to happen to me and my Sisters? Why would He let us go through such pain when we only try to help others and to serve Him? When is enough, enough?"

I sat for a moment and knew the words would be hard for her to hear, but they were true. I reminded her of how

God sent His only Son to become man and to die for our salvation. How Christ had come to serve, not to be served. I pointed to a Crucifix on the wall, and reminded her we were to live by His example. Christ gave everything for us, and in return He asks we give everything for others. Her soft eyes welled up with tears and she nodded her head agreeing. I hadn't told her anything that she didn't already understand. But often times we all need to hear from another what we already know in our heart.

My wife and I sat on each side of her and placed our hands on her shoulder and prayed with her for a short time. This wonderful woman seemed so frail, so tired of the long battle.

When we had finished we took turns hugging her, thanking her for all of her years of struggle and examplism. Her tired eyes seemed somehow changed. A smile returned to her face. She explained that before we had started there was such a fog all around her, but that now there was a hole in the fog and she could see light.

Sister L is just one of many heroic, saintly people who we have met. Her story is hard to hear. In all we listened to 3 ½ hours of things that had happened to her in her 45+ years. I truly believe she is a living Saint.

Chapter 9

The next morning we were to meet with a Priest of the Underground Catholic Church who we were told has been imprisoned on numerous occasions and is related to a very popular Under Ground Bishop. Being a very popular underground Bishop is not at all a safe occupation in China. Most Underground Bishops have been repeatedly imprisoned, under house arrest, or been pressured to go against Catholic teaching. These modern day Saints live out their lives being persecuted for being faithful followers of Christ. We traveled to a mall for our meeting. The priest had explained that out in the open things were less likely to get dangerous. We traveled first by black taxi and then by subway and arrived at a very busy mall. Our translator then received a call and we were asked to go to the second floor coffee shop and wait. So after several cups of coffee and 20-30 anxious minutes, I noticed a gentleman who had passed by several times, he smiled as he passed and walked on by. Within a few minutes he was back. He removed his jacket and sunglasses and introduced himself. He explained that he was just being cautious for our sake. He said often times he is followed and the police interview anyone he is in contact with, so he was just helping us to avoid any unfortunate circumstances. He gave us a large amount of information which I cannot convey here. The information has to do with future visits and would put too many good and faithful followers of Christ in needless danger. I will tell you that it was quite a look into the very unordinary life of a priest who is constantly on the run from the government. After hearing this man speak I have an extreme amount of respect for his path in God's plan. Please, as you read this say a small prayer for him and the many like him - men and women religious, who spend their lives spreading the gospel in difficult circumstances, who truly risk their lives spreading God's message.

In closing I will say that I have never considered myself a missionary. I do know God will use each one of us in a different way. I know He will stretch us, if we allow Him to. He will expand our circumference. We often believe we know our place and we often define our own borders or areas of comfort. He will, if we allow Him to, widen those borders and take us to places we would never dream of. I will not say everything about this mission was the kind of food and lodging as one would have in a 5 STAR establishment. But the people we met were second to none I have ever been fortunate enough to have met. These exceptional examples of today's disciples are a true testimony of God's ongoing plan in action. At the end of a tough day of business here in the United States, when I get home and hear all of the disgusting news on television of our countries dept, crooked politicians, divorces of the elite couples, terrorist activities, and the like I close my eyes and picture those people who struggle everyday just for freedom - the freedom to learn about, to know and love God.

The name used as the author of this book is not my real name. I have since this mission been to China on other missions. Knowing the facts that were revealed to me has made me more conscious of the dangers that are present for the people I have met. Since I plan on continuing with missions to the People's Republic of China, I must not be named here within this book. I fear that the contacts I have already made and any of the future contacts could be placed in harm's way. I know that it is a reality, that should I be found out, my Visa application would be denied in the future.

Please know that the proceeds from sales of this book will be used to help the children of our Brothers and Sisters of Christ in China.

Chapter 10

I referred in the start of this book to a lesson on "Increasing the Circumference of your Life." I feel led to include that teaching below.

First, we need to look at our current state in life and of all the things that it consists of - the particular time, place, friendships, employment, geographical area and education that make up our individual snapshot of who we are at this very moment in time.

Next, we can (either chart on paper or in our heads) start to visualize and understand how small our world is around us. Not in the entire world, that is here for us to live in and have an effect on, but the very small piece of area that we actually are living this part of our lives in.

We start to become aware of what our comfort zones are. Through understanding our comfort zones, we start to understand better how we limit what we are willing to do. Christ used very ordinary fishermen to become fishers of men.

As we get a better picture of who we are, who we have chosen to become through our free will, we start to understand ourselves better. But old habits die hard.

At this point we need to sit quietly and ask God who HE wants us to be. We need to sit quietly and just let HIM have some of our attention.

I know that for many years my conversations with God were very, if not totally, one sided. I would be thanking HIM for something, or asking him for something. I realized through a teaching similar to this that I was rarely, if ever, just listening.

I began to practice just sitting in front of the Eucharist and I would ask, "What do you want of me? Who do you want me to be? Where would you have me go?" Then I would sit quietly and contemplate HIS answers.

I won't say here I would receive words from God Himself, or that angels would surround me and give distinct directions (I don't always hear angelic voices singing), but HE will let us know HIS will. I will say I am learning to ask for HIS guidance on a level I had never allowed before.

I began to see HIS guidance in the words of others. I started to focus more on getting out of my comfort zone and opening myself up to more opportunities to serve HIM.

Often times I would read a book and find some particular paragraph, or sentence that I felt I needed to hear. I would hear HIS voice in words from others.

The next step is really tough if you do it with sincerity. Ask the Holy Spirit to lead you down a narrow path. Ask God what you can do for HIM, not just once, but start to ask HIM through the day.

Here is a brief example: I remember driving by a Catholic Church in a nearby town. I felt an urge to stop and just say hello. I think HE loves it when we just pop in.

As I walked into the empty church I blessed myself and followed the incredible urge I felt to say out loud, "Hello Dad, I'm home."

I ask you to try it sometime. I will say I felt an incredible overwhelming sensation of love. I sat for a few moments and just enjoyed being in front of the Tabernacle.

As I started to leave, I stopped and looked back at the Brass Tabernacle and the red glass covered candle that was lit beside it. I said aloud. "If you need anything between here and home let me know."

I was 45 miles from home in an area that was fairly desolate. I slowed to a crawl when I noticed a young man walking along side of the highway heading the same direction I was, and pulling up beside him I rolled down the passenger side window. I asked in a loud voice, "Do you need a ride?" I will say this was an obvious fact since the young man had no luggage, no backpack, nothing that would mark him as a hitch hiker. He was wearing jeans, a tee shirt and some black work boots. He looked to be in his later teens and had his hair dyed blue and pink. Not at all the sort of young man you see in a country area in the middle of nowhere.

He jumped a bit at hearing my voice, but as he grabbed the door handle he said yes sir I would appreciate it.

He looked so very surprised. Then he totally shocked me.

He said, "Sir I was just watching a few of the other cars pass by and I said to myself, God you gave all of these people cars and I don't have anything not even a ride. And that's when you hollered at me."

I found out he was 18 years old and over 1,200 miles away from home. He had been left by a girl who had disappeared down the highway. He had no money, no credit cards, nothing but $.52 in change. He explained his grandpa was his only family and he could live there in Tennessee with him if he could only make it back there.

Soon we arrived in the city and I bought him a $184.00 bus ticket for Tennessee and gave him the $20.00 I had in my wallet for food since it would be a 28 hour ride. Did I mention that sometimes doing God's work costs monetarily?

I believe that God wants to stretch us; that HE wants to mold us into more than we are. I know He never gives us more than we can handle. I also know that HE gives us free will and often in our lives that very same free will gets us into trouble.

The following is a prayer that I was given during an hour of adoration. I use it often and will share it here:

My Lord, my God, my King, my Savior, my everything, lead me where you will and make of me what I need be. Let me speak the words you would have me speak. Let me write the words you would have me write and keep me out of your way. Make your will known to me, so that I may lead the life you will me to lead. When I fail, oh Lord, be patient with me, for I am not always the man/woman I should be. Please give me the grace to be the best son/daughter, man/woman, husband/wife, parent, friend, worker, example and most of all, Christian that I can be. Please forgive me for all the times in the past I have put my wants above others needs. Forgive me for any and all of my offenses against you. Let me have the vision of what I can do to help others. Give me patience and knowledge to help the young and the elderly. Let me recognize what is needed and guide me to completion of those tasks. I pray that you will help me become the best servant I can be. Give me the strength and courage to live life as you request. Lead me to the discipline necessary to complete whatever you have for me to do in the short time I am on this earth. Thank you for putting up with me, for creating me, for giving me this chance to live. Most of all thank you for your sacrifice, for dying so that I may live forever with you. May I learn to praise you in all that I do and in all that I am. Amen.

If we can learn to open our minds and make a conscience decision to give our present circumstances and circumference of our life over to God, He will make HIS will known to us. Let us knock and let that door be opened. But let us also walk through that door and see where God is leading us. Let us add something now in this very moment in time that will allow us to open our life more fully to the Holy Spirit and HIS will.

Heavenly Father, I give you permission to take over my life. I will try from this moment on to ask what you have that needs doing. I will pray for my ears to open to your loving guidance in my life. Drain me of all that I don't need, of the habits, the materials and thoughts that aren't of you and replace them with your will for me. Now sit quietly with your eyes closed for a moment and just relax into HIS presence.

Repeat this exercise over and over in the days and weeks to come and know that God doesn't give empty promises, HE will answer. Be ready to listen to HIS voice in all the things and people around you, test each one with discernment and know that HE loves you.

www.ingramcontent.com/pod-product-compliance
Lightning Source LLC
Chambersburg PA
CBHW031414040426
42444CB00005B/568